Lecture on Mormonism

By Benjamin M. Palmer

ISBN: 978-1-63118-637-0

Mormon History Series

Other Books in this Series and Related Titles

Pearl of Great Price by Joseph Smith (978-1-63118-539-7)

The Angel of the Prairies or A Dream of the Future: Mormon History Series
By Elder Parley Parker Pratt (978-1-63118-541-0)

A Manuscript on Far West by Reed Peck (978-1-63118-544-1)

The Story of Mormonism by James E Talmage (978-1-63118-543-4)

Interesting Account of Several Remarkable Visions: Mormon History Series
By Orson Pratt (978-1-63118-553-3)

An Address to All Believers in Christ Elder David Whitmer (978-1-63118-545-8)

The Book of John Whitmer by John Whitmer (978-1-63118-554-0)

The Philosophy of Mormonism by James E Talmage (978-1-63118-542-7)

The Book of Abraham: Mormon History by George Reynolds (978-1-63118-540-3)

The Testament of Abraham by Abraham (978-1-63118-441-3)

Private Diary of Joseph Smith 1832-1834 (978-1-63118-546-5)

Times and Seasons Volume 1, Numbers 1-3 (978-1-63118-555-7)

Times and Seasons Volume 1, Numbers 4-6 (978-1-63118-556-4)

The Evening and Morning Star Volume 1, Numbers 1 & 2 (978-1-63118-547-2)

The Evening and Morning Star Volume 1, Numbers 3 & 4 (978-1-63118-548-9)

The Evening and Morning Star Volume 1, Numbers 5 & 6 (978-1-63118-549-6)

The Book of the Nephilim by Enoch (978-1-63118-627-1)

The Lost Book of Noah by Noah (978-1-63118-624-0)

The Secrets of Enoch by Enoch (978-1-63118-449-9)

The Book of the Watchers by Enoch (978-1-63118-416-1)

Audio Versions are also available on Audible, Amazon and Apple

Other Books in this Series and Related Titles

The Hidden Mysteries of Christianity by Annie Besant (978–1–63118–534–2)

Rosicrucian Rules, Secret Signs, Codes and Symbols by various (978-1-63118-488-8)

History and Teachings of the Rosicrucians by W W Westcott &c (978-1-63118-487-1)

Freemasonry and the Egyptian Mysteries by C. W. Leadbeater (978-1-63118-456-7)

The Sepher Yetzirah and the Qabalah by M P Hall (978-1-63118-481-9)

The Psalms of Solomon by King Solomon (978-1-63118-439-0)

The Historic, Mythic and Mystic Christ by Annie Besant (978–1–63118–533–5)

Masonic and Rosicrucian History by M P Hall & H Voorhis (978-1-63118-486-4)

The Kabbalah of Masonry & Related Writings by E Levi &c (978-1-63118-453-6)

Some Deeper Aspects of Masonic Symbolism by A E Waite (978-1-63118-461-1)

Masonic Symbolism of King Solomon's Temple by A Mackey &c (978-1-63118-442-0)

The Old Past Master by Carl H Claudy (978-1-63118-464-2)

The Influence of Pythagoras on Freemasonry and Other Essays (978-1-63118-404-8)

The Mysteries of Freemasonry & the Druids by various (978-1-63118-444-4)

Masonic Symbolism of the Apron & the Altar by various (978-1-63118-428-4)

The Book of Wisdom of Solomon by King Solomon (978-1-63118-502-1)

Masonic Symbolism of Easter and the Christ in Masonry (978-1-63118-434-5)

The Odes of Solomon by King Solomon (978-1-63118-503-8)

Ancient Mysteries and Secret Societies by M P Hall (978-1-63118-410-9)

The Golden Verses of Pythagoras: Five Translations (978-1-63118-479-6)

Freemasonry & Catholicism by Max Heindel (978-1-63118-508-3)

A Few Masonic Sermons by A. C. Ward &c (978-1-63118-435-2)

Audio versions are also available on Audible, Amazon and Apple

Table of Contents

A LECTURE

DELIVERED BEFORE THE

MERCANTILE LIBRARY ASSOCIATION

OF

CHARLESTON, S. C.

BY

B. M. PALMER, D. D.

JANUARY 26, 1853.

COLUMBIA, S. C.
PRINTED BY I. C. MORGAN.
1853

LECTURE ON MORMONISM

One of the most striking and significant events of the present century, is the rise and spread of Mormonism. All the chapters of its changeful history possess the interest of the most stirring romance. The incidents thicken so fast, the plot becomes so complex, and withal, the developments are so vast and unexpected, that we hold our breath in continual surprise, in threading our way through the narrative of this singular delusion.

The world has long been familiar with Heresiarchs who have gone off upon some perversion of Christian doctrine: but the schools they have established claim still a connection with the Church out of whose bosom they spring; and the leprous taint has not unfrequently extended from the branch and defiled the trunk. But since the sixth century, no original impostor had arisen, claiming immediate inspiration from God, and establishing a new dispensation of truth. To make this novelty more startling, it was reserved for this age, and for this country, to give birth to the new Prophet: an age advanced beyond all others in the natural sciences, by which imposture may be detected; and a country having the most thoroughly practical population upon the globe. We may, in the sequel, perhaps, find in these very circumstances, which excite our wonder, the elements from which to work out the solution of this great social and religious problem.— But at the first glance, it strikes one with astonishment that in the middle of the nineteenth century, and in this enlightened, Christian land, so clumsy an imposture should be attempted and succeed. That an obscure and illiterate man, without position or character even in his own humble circle, should make the stupendous claim of inspiration from God; should travesty the sacred and antique dialect of the Bible, and foist his wretched compositions upon the world, with all the sanction of a new revelation; and that unauthenticated by any signs or wonders, such as have always attested a divine Herald, he should be accepted upon his own naked testimony as a true prophet.—these are statements we must receive, however antecedently improbable, simply because they are facts of contemporaneous history. It may not surprise us that this upstart religion, excommunicating the whole Christian church in one sweeping anathema, and superseding her canonical writings with its own tripping inspiration, should suffer violence and persecution. But after enduring protracted horrors, such as only the religious sentiment can outlive, that the miserable refugees should assemble, at a concerted signal, across a thousand miles of pathless desert, and in three short revolving seasons, should plant fields, erect mills, establish schools, build cities, and institute all the arts of civilized life,—in a word, that they should lay the foundation of a new empire, and with one hand upon the articles of confederation, should with the other be almost knocking for admission into this family of States: these are achievements over-topping the fictions of Eastern romance; at least, resembling more the gorgeous dreams of Arabian fancy, than the sober facts of real life. But the cap-stone of this wonderful history, the climax of its marvels, is, that in a religion not old to wear a beard, and in an empire not yet out of swaddling clothes, we should be presented with the only

American State-church, and witness an effort partially successful to re-produce the Asiatic type of civilization.

I have thus, gentlemen, sketched the contour of Mormonism, and sought to place you at a point from which you may take in, at one view, both its pretensions and its achievements, in order, if possible, to abate your merriment when I announce it as the theme of the present lecture. Perhaps in uncasing this stupendous fraud, the moralist, the divine, the statesman, and the political economist, may each find, in his own department, material for profound speculation.

It is never easy to form a correct estimate of religious impostors. The deceit and falsehood which mark their course, seem scarcely consistent with the religious sentiment that must underlie the character. The great controversy, for example, whether Mohammed was a fanatic or an impostor, proceeds upon the supposed incompatibility of the two; yet. their co-existence is needed to solve the facts of the case. We cannot explain the origin of a religious imposture, without supposing the religious element to be awakened, however it may be afterwards debauched and misdirected. The history of error abundantly shows that the most vicious principles will often mingle with the religious instincts of men, who are driven under this double impulse into the most riotous excesses. The original exciting cause may be slight enough; but the hallucination once entertained of miraculous correspondence with Heaven, an unscrupulous or ignorant conscience will not long hesitate at fraud in accomplishing the holy mission; and when success shall have consecrated the cheat, the impostor becomes fully ensnared in his own lie, and easily credits to supernatural revelation the suggestions of his own fancy. Joseph Smith, the founder of the Mormon sect, is dogmatically pronounced an impostor by thousands who do not stop to inquire how far he may also have been an enthusiast; or to solve the query whether it be possible to control the religious convictions of our fellow men, without a previous excitation of our own religious nature. The biography of this remarkable person opens with the account of his deep spiritual distress during an exciting religious revival through which he passed while still a youth. Perplexed in his choice between conflicting sects and creeds, he was for a time in that state of indecision in which multitudes vibrate between superstition and skepticism. While perhaps upon the verge of infidelity, he swung to the opposite pole, and conceived the project of founding a church, whose comprehensive creed should harmonize all sects, and swallow up dissent: and this lively suggestion of his own mind, a heated imagination may easily have coined into a vision of God. Seven years however elapse, before this bold conception embodies itself in a detailed scheme. While "the vision tarries," the nascent Prophet relapses, if the story be true, into the vagrant habits of his early life, which show him to be constitutionally of a deeply superstitious turn. By the aid of seer-stones and hazel-rods, he had gained no small reputation as a money-digger. Certainly, if he failed to track the secret veins of silver, he did not fail to sound the depths of human credulity. At the end of seven years, he is prepared to enter upon prophetical functions, and announces a new revelation, whose origin forms a curious record in the annals of literary forgery. A disabled clergyman, Mr. Spalding, residing in Ohio, amused the heavy hours occasioned by chronic disease, and indulged a creative fancy in penning a historical romance, entitled "the Manuscript found." Seizing on the familiar idea that the North American Indians are lineal descendants of the lost ten tribes of Israel, it purported to trace those tribes from the time when history loses them, and to describe their settlement on this continent, their division into existing clans, with their wars and mode of living. As the fiction was bold and lively, it was read in successive portions by the author's friends, as rapidly as he composed. His premature death prevented its publication; and it lay for many years amongst dusty papers, almost forgotten. By what legerdemain it came into the hands of Joseph Smith, none but he could disclose, while it was his interest to conceal. Too many witnesses, however, attest the substantial identity of the published book of Mormon with this manuscript, to admit a doubt of the plagiarism: and the mysterious disappearance of the document from the family archives, affords presumption of the theft.

When the mind is quickened by enthusiasm, the slightest incidents become tributary to the one idea which fills and masters it. The romance of Mr. Spalding gave to Smith the key-note of his imposture. The golden plates which he professed to dig by divine direction from the hill-side at Cumorrah, taught that Christ, after his ascension into Heaven, again descended and planted his Church among the lost tribes of Israel on this continent—that these, having forfeited his favour by their apostacy, were given up to be destroyed by their enemies,—and that by the last of their prophets, these records were deposited in the earth, to be brought forth in the fulness of time by a Gentile. The favoured restorer of these ancient oracles is the

Mormon Prophet, who is divinely taught to translate the same, and to restore the suspended animation of this long-lost church. 'The first proselytes to this new faith were the different members of his father's family; who, however, did not render the service of two individuals, Pratt and Rigdon, who were the next converts. With the assistance of these, especially of the latter, the organization of the sect is further matured, and the new doctrines extensively promulged. A temporary gathering of the early converts is made at Kirtland, in Ohio; though, from the beginning, the policy seems to have been to settle his colony upon the frontiers of civilization. It would be the repetition of a familiar tale to recite their settlement in Missouri, or to detail the violence which drove them to find a refuge in Illinois. The building of their city, Nauvoo, and the erection of a magnificent temple,—the murder of their prophet, while under the sacred guardianship of the law, by a perfidious mob—their expulsion from Nauvoo—the virtual confiscation of their property—the destruction of their temple—the report of all this has long since come to every ear. The death of Smith at this juncture was not, perhaps, injurious to the Mormon interest. It set the seal of martyrdom to a system which to many might otherwise have been only a crazy superstition; it released the prophet himself from the dizzy height to which he had climbed—and which none after him was expected to reach—and it made room for the ascendency of a broader and more practical mind in Brigham Young, the new President. Their successive expulsions from Missouri and Illinois sufficiently proved, what might indeed have been demonstrated *a priori*, the impracticability of two communities, organically different in their social structure, living peaceably intermingled. Emigration to a country where they should altogether escape the pressure of a surrounding population, was now an established necessity. Never was an emigration better planned or conducted. Explorers bring back an account of the great Salt Lake Valley, in Utah, the locality precisely suited for the "manifest destiny" before them. Situated midway between the Mississippi and the great Pacific, they would be far enough removed from both, yet sufficiently nigh to connect their fortunes with the States that must eventually skirt either ocean. A fertile territory, capable, when artificially irrigated, and under perfect culture, of sustaining a population of four thousand to a square mile, and large enough to embrace a million of souls, invited their entrance. This valley, too, like that of the Abyssinian Prince, is insulated at every point of the compass—if not by walls of rock, at least by inhospitable, arid deserts, and untimbered slopes—which might repress the advancing tide of settlers, and leave the saints without restraint to work out their high mission. From the moment that emigration to this chosen spot was decided on, the deepest practical wisdom marks all their movements, disclosing the presiding genius of a master mind. A party of pioneers is first sent forward to occupy some portion of the waste land westward of the States, with instructions to put in a crop which might sustain the larger body soon to take up the line of march. The same wise precaution was used the following season, before arriving at their new home, when the emigrants found a harvest waiting for their sickles, the fruit of the toils of a similar advance-guard. At once, a city is symmetrically laid out, a site selected for the temple, a bowery erected for temporary worship, fields measured off, and put under cultivation, furnaces put in blast, mills built upon water courses, canals dug for the circulation of water, and the whole industry of a tried and hardy people supervised by one controlling mind. The effect of this concentrated and regulated labor is told in the stupendous results already hinted—all danger of famine is warded off, and a sufficient store provided for the saints who should obey the bugle-call of their chieftain, bidding them from afar to this land of promise. A chain of settlements is marked out, and cities founded, as stepping-stones to the Pacific coast; a Provisional government is constituted, and Utah distinctly recognised as a territory in the halls of Congress.

This rude outline of their fortunes and progress will perhaps suffice to fix your interest upon this people, and prepare the way for such reflections as I may be able to submit.

The first fact which arrests the attention of one who looks into the details of this imposture, is the close parallel between the Mormon and the Arabian prophet. The resemblance, indeed, is so obvious that, in common parlance, Smith is designated as "the American Mahomet:" though this title may be assigned only upon the general ground that both sought to found a new religion, and substantially by the same method; both feigned to be inspired, and both palmed upon the world a new revelation from heaven. It would subserve no useful end to trace the minute coincidences between the two; but I cannot, perhaps, better exhibit the Mormon system than by running the parallel in some of the more prominent points.

I. *Mormonism and Mohammedism are both clumsy attempts to reconcile and unite conflicting creeds.* This idea is the seed from which the two religions unquestionably germinated. It has been already stated that Smith conceived his project immediately after his religious convictions were powerfully awakened, and when he was sorely puzzled to make his election between churches, which perhaps indecently canvassed for his favor. When the angel announced to him that there was no true Church upon earth, it was probably only the skeptical doubt of his own mind putting on a fanatical disguise. The religious element was not, however, to be extinguished thus, by placing it in the exhausted receiver of a negative infidelity. His very superstition drove him to fill the "aching void" with a faith of some sort; and his inventive genius sought to compound existing systems, and to frame a Church which should present attractions to every sect. He evidently jars as slightly against the branches of the Christian Church, by which he was surrounded, as was consistent with the exclusive claims arrogated to his own. The mission of Christ is not denied. On the contrary, predictions were produced from the Nephitic records, in which the Messiah is announced by name, as distinctly as was the Persian Cyrus by Isaiah of old. The Church, as established in the Apostolic age, is admitted to be pure, but alleged to have so changed God's covenant, and corrupted his ordinances, as to be now wholly apostate. The Bible is recognised as "the foundation book"—only charged with interpolations which the Mormon seer was commissioned to detect. Its authority is not absolutely impugned, but succeeding revelations must be admitted to an equal share of its supremacy. More particular deference is shown to it, in glossing certain passages of the prophetical writings, especially of Ezekiel, to lend support to the new revelation. Some of its peculiar doctrines, as the

Millennium, and the Resurrection, are incorporated into his creed; though the former is pushed to the utmost extravagance of Millenarian speculation, and the latter undertakes to define what are the properties of the spiritual body. The sacraments of the New Testament, Baptism and the Lord's Supper, are received, and the former practised according to the views of the most rigid immersionists, and supposed to secure infallibly the remission of sins. The evangelical terms, faith, repentance, obedience, atonement, forgiveness, are freely employed, though for the most part in an obscure and mystical sense.

In another section will be exhibited the clear recognition of the Jewish Economy. Indeed, the effort is most apparent to fuse the first and second dispensations into one, and to present Mormonism as the amalgam of the two. A sa symbol of this, the spirits of Moses and Elias, as representatives of the one, and the spirits of Peter, James and John, as representatives of the other, lent the sauction of their presence at his baptism, and covered the necessary irregularity of receiving it at the hands of the neophyte, Cowdery. This eclectic system takes a wider range, and smacks with the flavor of almost every Pagan superstition and mystical school upon earth. Not wishing to anticipate what will be more appropriately noticed in another connection, it is sufficient here to glance at the Gnostic dogma of æons in the Mormon "Principles of Element," or matter—the Pantheism which, beginning with making God a man, very consistently ends with making man a God—and the Persian idea of transmigration of souls in accomplishing their probation. A simple reference to these heterogeneous opinions suffices to show that Mormonism is truly an "Olla Podrida" of all the religions and superstitions upon the globe.

Let us now turn back the shadow upon the dial-plate of time at least twelve hundred years, and share the meditations of the prophet of the sixth century, in his lonely cave on Mt. Hera. He looks forth upon the tribes of Arabia, whom a haughty spirit of independence, nourished through centuries of personal and civil freedom, had made the free-thinkers of their day. Some, weaded to the ancient Sabian idolatry, did homage to the hosts of heaven, or to the angels and their images; others bowed with Magian reverence before fire as the appropriate symbol of the Deity. Every pious fraud must have its secret foundation in some religious idea; and Mohammed was enough in contact with a purer faith, to seize the truth of God's essential unity, against which all these systems impinged. To his bold, reflecting mind, this fundamental truth loomed up with a grandeur which frowned awfully upon the paltry superstitions of the idolater. His soul may have caught fire, as the thought flashed upon him to reclaim these wretched Polytheists to the great platform of all Natural and Revealed Religion, the existence of one supreme and spiritual God. If. on the other hand, he turned from the idolatries of the Pagan, the dissensions and corruptions of Christianity were little less repulsive. The mystery of iniquity, predicted in Apostolic times, had already commenced to work; and in the sixth century, the concurrent testimony of all historians represents the worship of saints and images as carried already to the highest pitch—and it is easy to see how a Pagan mind, looking at Christianity through this medium, should misconceive even the doctrine of the Trinity, as contravening the essential unity of the Divine nature. Not only so, the heresies and conflicts of this period were so loud and bitter, fomented by bishops and emperors, and anathemas rung so fierce from councils, as naturally to bewilder a mind not indoctrinated to perceive the shades of difference in theological opinion. This, then, was doubtless the religious germ of the Arabian imposture. In the language of a learned writer, quoted in Sale's Preliminary Discourse, "the general design of the Koran seems to be to unite the professors of the three different religions then followed in the populous country of Arabia, who, for the most part, lived promiscuously, and wandered without guides, the far greater number being idolaters, and the rest Jews and Christians mostly of erroneous and heterodox belief, in the worship of one eternal, invisible God.

In all religions, true or false, there is one reigning idea, the nucleus about which the different parts may crystallize, in regular logical process. In the Mohammedan scheme the dominant pretension is that of "replanting the only true and ancient religion professed by Adam, Noah, Abraham, Moses, Jesus, and all the prophets." The supreme idea in the Mormon imposture seems to be the restoration of the Church to its ancient apostolic powers—the gift of faith, discerning of spirits, prophecy, revelation, visions, healings, tongues, interpretation of tongues—and the recovery of certain lost ordinances, such as the Priesthood with its sacrifices, and the laying on of hands with the gift of the Holy Ghost. The Arabian, like the American prophet, recognised the mission of Moses and of Christ, and compiled largely from the Christian and Jewish Scriptures in framing his own revelation. Moses need not leave his seat, nor Christ his throne, if only Mohammed be admitted to their company, and be crowned as the last of the prophets.

II. The second feature of resemblance between the two systems is, *that Judaism is assumed as mainly the basis of both.* Mohammed began his career with sentiments of high consideration for the Jews; though his disappointment in gaining them as proselytes, through the proverbial tenacity of their faith, eventually converted this regard into rancour. It is possible that the heart of the Ishmaelite may have softened towards the children of Abraham, as both recognised in their flesh the seal of an early brotherhood. The Jews too, whom the wild freedom of Arabia had nourished into consequence, were the great confessors of that sublime truth which now filled the reason and the fancy of the reformer. Judaism thus unquestionably furnished the ground-doctrine of the Koran, and gave to Islamism its rallying cry. Mohammed displayed great wisdom in restricting his doctrinal articles within so narrow a compass. Only the thorny doctrine of absolute predestination was likely to entice to metaphysical discussion; and it did give ample exercise to the dialectic skill of future doctors. Easy credence was given to the simple and fundamental postulate of the divine unity, while the practical devotions of the Moslem were included in the four particulars of prayer, fasting, alms and pilgrimages. In all of these a remarkable resemblance is traced to Jewish institutions, though it must be confessed to the institutions of Rabbinical, much more than of primitive, Judaism. Five times a day the Muezzim sound the hours of prayer, when the Musselman bows with the same posture of adoration towards Mecca, as the Jew towards the Holy. City. The purifications of the one, performed with scrupulous exactness, find their type in the ritual ablutions of the other. The legal alms, being an exact per centage of all the Mohammedan calls his own, bear a close affinity to the tithes anciently paid into the hands of Levi. A similar distinction of meats, and the same prohibition of usury, occur in both religions. The same superstitious value attached to excessive fasting, which met our Saviour's rebuke among the Jews, marks this religious duty as prescribed by Mohammed. The pilgrimage to Mecca, though a relic of old Arabian Paganism, may, perhaps, have been sanctioned in the impostor's. mind, by the solemn assemblages of Israel in the temple, at their great feasts. It would be tedious to follow the parallel in the Mohammedan notions of heaven, and their doctrine of angels. Any one at all curious on this point, may easily find guides who will conduct him through vast collections of Jewish and Moslem legends, the analogy between the two being apparent at every step in the comparison.

Mormonism is a far more servile imitation of Judaism, as it incorporates even those peculiar features which the introduction of Christianity rendered obsolete. It was a bold stroke of policy to reconstruct the old Jewish platform, as the basis of the new imposture. By connecting the North American Indians with the ancient Israel of God, and inventing a history for them so full of dignity and privilege as the Book of Mormon disclosed, he hoped to flatter the pride of this simple people, who might be thought easily persuaded to welcome their ancient, honorable, resuscitated Church. On the other hand, the Mormon apostles take sufficient care that so handsome a compliment to Judaism shall not escape the notice of the Rabbies, the world over—an act of reverence that should subdue the prejudices of this hitherto invincible sect. Meanwhile, all Christendom was to be won by the distinct testimony borne to the Messiahship of Jesus, and the revival of those supernatural gifts which graced the Church in Apostolic days.

The most prominent feature of Judaism, the Priesthood of Aaron, is transferred to this new dispensation, and is curiously coupled with the higher priesthood of Melchisedek. It is distinctly held that a priesthood is essential to the being of a Church; and one writer distinctly implies that upon the completion of their temple, animal sacrifices are to be renewed for the daily sins of the people. Tithes are paid, as of old—the proselyte giving one tenth of his entire substance, and ever after a tithe of his labor, time and income, accumulating a fund for the advancement of public interests. The temple built at Nauvoo, with its baptistic laver, resting upon twelve oxen elaborately carved of marble, sought to emulate the glory and splendor of Solomon's. Their travels, painfully accomplished through the desert to their western home, find a prototype in the Exode from Egypt, and the long journey of the Israelites, through the wilderness, to the land of promise. The literal gathering of the scattered Jews to Palestine, and the re-establishment of the ancient ritual in its splendor—their conversion by the glorious manifestation of Jesus in the heavens—the assemblage of the latter-day saints in the

American Zion—the re-marriage of continents and islands as at the creation, and the casting up of a highway on the united earth, between the two Jerusalems—their being caught. up to heaven, while the earth shall be purged by fire, to descend and remain forever on the new earth—all these doctrines, firmly believed, abundantly indicate the leaven of Judaism pervading the New Church creed, and confirm the position before taken, that Judaism forms the chief basis of the Mormon Church.

III. *A third parallelism is found in the claim urged by both, to progressive Revelation.* Mohammed taught that "God, in divers ages of the world, gave revelations of his will in writing to several prophets"—to Adam, Seth, Enoch, Abraham, Moses, David, Jesus, and himself. He being the last, prophecy is henceforth sealed up, and no further revelations are to be expected. Those which were made to him came in parcels as exigencies arose—and if one contradicted another, the first was considered abrogated. The canon was complete at his death, and none of the Caliphs who succeeded him ventured to assume his prophetic mantle, or to re-open personal correspondence with the Deity.

The claims of Smith are vastly more extravagant, and *development* is represented as the peculiar glory of the latter-day Church. He did not, like his Arabian prototype, prudently seal the prophetic roll at his own death; but left the sacred gift as the perpetual inheritance of the saints. "New revelation," says Orson Pratt, one of the Mormon Apostles, "is the very life and soul of the religion of Heaven," and without it "there is an end to the very existence of the Church of Christ on earth; there is an end to salvation in the celestial kingdom." Revelations are necessary to the calling of officers, to instruction in the nature of their duties—necessary to the conveyance of consolation or reproof—to escape from judgments—and to the entire edification of the saints. The sufficiency of all past revelations for the guidance of the Church is stoutly denied. In accordance with these views, Smith, like Mohammed, to the end of his career extricated himself from all dilenmmas by a new disclosure of the Divine will. His successor, Brigham Young, with the shrewdness which. marks his whole administration, is extremely chary of these prophetic announcements. Not enjoying the prestige, with Smith, of having opened this correspondence with Deity, he prudently excuses the sluggishness of his own vaticinations, upon the plea that the revelations of the first prophet have cut out work for several years ahead. The practical judgement of the first President would doubtless close altogether this door to fanaticism, if it were possible to contravene the will of the prophet. But a secret, controlling Providence is manifest in Smith's leaving that fatal gift, by which this gross imposture shall be made finally to convict and stultify itself.

IV. *A still more obvious resemblance is found in the sensual element introduced into both.* It needs few words to establish this charge against the Arabian imposture. The world knows that Mohammed practised, and that the Koran sanctions, polygamy; yet it should be always borne in mind that this social enormity existed before his day, and prevailed generally throughout the East. All that is fairly. chargeable upon Islamism, is, that it sanctioned a plurality of wives. So far from originating it, Mohammed recognised it as a permanent feature of Eastern society, and rather restricted than expanded the privilege to his followers. It was not lawful to exceed a given number, though by special favor his own harem was enlarged to the extent of his desires. From the charge, however, of ministering to the appetites, by providing a sensual Paradise for the faithful after death, he cannot so easily be acquitted. Delightful fruits, exquisite wines, the richest apparel, a profusion of rubies and pearls, sumptuous abodes, black-eyed maidens, and above all, perpetual youth giving zest to enjoyments which no indulgence can blunt; all these form, not the language of parable figuring the inconceivable spiritual blessedness of the faithful, but with offensive literalness, they minutely address every sense and appetite, both of body and of soul. The influence of these sensual rewards, upon the warm blood and quick fancy of oriental nations, can scarcely be measured; especially when obtained upon the easy condition of perfect devotion to the Prophet of Allah.

It was denied that polygamy formed one of the features of Mormonism, as long as the infant sect was thought unable to sustain the shock of public indignation. A Church, whose boast is development, may be expected to put forth new traits, when the credulity of its devotees will warrant the disclosure. But whether the spiritual-wife system is a new revelation, or whether it was one of the esoteric doctrines from the beginning, it is now avowed and defended as an integral part of the scheme. No feature of this new dispensation appears so curious or adventurous, as this attempt to disturb and to change the organic law upon which all society with us is constructed. If there be one exponent of Christian civilization, it is the position of woman in the domestic and social circle. For ages her melancholy doom was either to toil as a drudge for an insolent master, or, what was scarcely less repugnant to her nature, to be the passive instrument of his pleasures. During that middle age which marks the transition to modern civilization, she was sported as a toy; but the veil of seclusion was not yet drawn, nor did she walk with man, his friend and equal, in the open paths of life. But where the Bible blesses the marriage vow, it founds upon the union of a single pair the constitution of a happy family. The woman walks hand in hand with her lawful spouse, the sole mistress of his heart, sharing his sorrow and his joy; they breast together the fortunes of life, and even in death are still united in the affectionate remembrance of grateful descendants. Mormonism impudently strives to reproduce the Asiatic type of civilization. It scoffs at the deference which the Christian world pays to the female sex, and stigmatizes it as "Gentile gallantry;" it teaches that no woman can gain admission into the Heavenly Kingdom, but through the introduction of her husband; it "seals," to use its own cant phrase, as many wives to one man as he may wish to maintain, and graduates a man's rank in the celestial Paradise by the largeness of his retinue. Like Mohammed, the Mormon advocate pleads the example of ancient patriarchs—but more gross than he, no restriction is placed upon this secret sealing, but the ability to render a suitable provision for the multiplied households.

V. *The last comparison which I shall institute relates to the union of civil and ecclesiastical power, in the two systems.* 'To elaborate the proof of this in regard to the religion of Islam, would be to trifle with the patience, if not with the intelligence, of this audience. After his flight to Medina, Mohammed own his mission to be the propagation of the new faith by fire and sword. Drawing into precedent the exterminating wars of Israel with the devoted inhabitants of Canaan, "there is no God but Allah" was transformed from the peaceful symbol of religious devotees into the battle-cry of an armed soldiery. Before his death, nearly all the tribes of Arabia had sent embassies of allegiance to the conqueror of Mecca, and idolatry had given place to the deism of the Koran. The Caliphs who succeeded to the enterprise were men born to empire, possessed of rare courage, and inspired with the patience and self-denial which belong to religious zeal. The campaigns, planned with wonderful forecast, were conducted with the precipitate intrepidity characteristic of fanaticism. In the reign of Omar—we cite from Gibbon—ten years saw thirty-six thousand cities or castles dismantled, four thousand churches or temples demolished, and fourteen hundred mosques erected. Within a century after the Hegira, the young moon which lighted the exile in his solitary flight, filled to a glorious orb; and the Crescent waved in triumph over the plains of Syria, the steppes of Persia, the sands of Africa, and the fertile deltas of Egypt. The desolating flood of conquest swept on, and, washing the Pillars of Hercules, passed from Asia into Europe, soon covered the Spanish Peninsula, and finally broke its fury at the foot of the Pyrennees, when the hardy German race first breasted the mighty surge.

The Koran is not only the corner-stone of the Saracen Empire, but its precepts constitute the fundamental part of the civil law. The Caliph, as successor of Mohammed, which the term indicates, unites in his person the royal and sacerdotal functions. No higher evidence can he demanded of a Church-state than the union of the. crosier with the sceptre, the monarch and the priest.

In Mormonism the civil power is much more built into the ecclesiastical; nor is there the least inclination to blink the union of the two. As the whole religion and polity emanated from Joseph Smith, he was, during life, the head of all power, and gave laws with the authority of a dictator. The hierarchy of the latter-day Church is very complex. It consists of a Presidency supported by a cabinet of counsellors, called the High Council of the Twelve. Next is the travelling Apostolic College of the Twelve, after the New Testament model, who are witnesses to Jew and Gentile, over all the world; then the Seventy, with a whole army of priests, elders, bishops, teachers, deacons, &c.,—each order constituting a court, the higher having appellate jurisdiction over the lower. The cope-stone of the entire structure is the Presidency of the High Priesthood. He disburses the public fund accumulated from the payment of tithes; his permission in every case of "sealing" gains him access as a confidential adviser into every household; and the new revelations dispensed from heaven enable him always to speak with "the nod and sanction of a God." It is hard to see how more absolute power could be vested in any ruler. And the wonderful results attained in the Salt Lake Valley, in the short space of three years, are in evidence that the influence and power thus vested have been practically exerted, and that the

Presidency of Brigham Young does not exist alone upon parchment.

In tracing this parallel, I am far from wishing to degrade Mohammed to the intellectual or-moral level of Joseph Smith. He was unquestionably cast in a far nobler mould, and, impostor as he was, never descended to the pitiful forgery of his modern rival. Bald, and even vicious, as his religion was, it was still in advance of the idolatry which it supplanted. So far as he reclaimed his country-men from polytheism to the recognition of the invisible and spiritual God, he was indisputably a reformer; and full of puerilities as the Koran may be, it never drivels in the contemptible blasphemy of the "Book of Mormon." As a statesman, too, he pushed his country forward, and gave a dignity to her name, such as she never before enjoyed. He found the tribes of Arabia rudely independent and dissociated; he gave them a bond of union, and founded a compact and powerful empire, whose history is illustrated with deeds of prowess equal to any recorded in the annals of the most romantic chivalry. Viewed either as a religious or political movement, Mohammedism was a step in advance of the past; one stage, at least so far as Arabia was concerned, in the mighty march of the race of man. Mormonism, on the contrary, is an open apostacy from the highest type of civilization to that which is most beastly—a rejection of the most spiritual religion in favor of that which is most gross and material—a bold step, taken backward, in defiance of all the lessons of history, and in the face of a people the most intelligent and free upon the globe.

It is time now to shift the scene, and to present Mormonism in its relations to the present, as well as in its resemblance to the past. All those enterprises which combine numbers in their execution may be taken as exponents of the age in which they occur. However they may be, in their origin, the mintage of a single brain, yet the elective affinity, by which they attract adherents on every side, must express some trait of the time.

1. Mormonism, for example, has *borrowed from Christianity its aggressive feature,* and sends its missionaries likewise to gather prosclytes from all parts of the earth. Christianity is the first system of religion that sought to propagate itself by the labors of evangelists travelling or residing in foreign countries. Judaism was a stationary system. Planted in the centre of the old world, its light gleamed far and wide into the surrounding darkness. Through its transparent symbols it held up the truth to the gaze of the nations; but it went forth upon no mission of propagation, and was anchored by its ordinances and ritual to the land of Palestine. In like manner, the various systems of Polytheism were local, and animated with no spirit of propagandism. Each country had its own divinities; and as a miserable substitute for one, supreme omnipresent being, the number of local deities was so, multiplied that Polytheism was likely to break down of its weight. So far from excluding the Gods of a conquered territory, conquest only served to enlarge the boundaries of idolatry; until, as in the Pantheon at Rome, thousands of divinities were assembled in friendly embrace, representatives of the diversified worship of mankind. But Christianity came forth, with her commission written on her

brow by her Divine founder: "Go into all the world, and disciple all nations." This makes her essentially an aggressive body—carrying her faith by peaceful and persuasive means to every quarter of the globe. Her history is, to a large extent, the record of her missionary labors; and those who breathe most largely her spirit, are most earnest in seeking the fulfilment of this her great commission.

This feature, hitherto characteristic only of the Christian religion, has been engrafted upon the Mormon superstition; and no fitter illustration can be afforded of the despotic power of their rulers than is afforded by the manner in which the missionaries are sent forth. Upon three days' notice, often, they are called by the will of their superiors to leave their business and their families, and to go forth without purse or scrip, ignorant even of the languages which they are to use, trusting to Providence for their support. With a craftiness, as well as with a despotism, worthy of Ignatins Loyola, the most ambitious and inquisitive of the sect are chosen for this work; who are not only flattered into superior devotion by this signal mark of confidence, but are confirmed the more in the Mormon faith as they are compelled to defend it, and find abundant labors in which to expend the superfluous energy which it might not be so easy to check at home. It is already the boast of Mormonism, that brief and troubled as its history has been, there are few prominent countries in which its. Gospel has not been proclaimed. In Germany, Italy, France, Norway, Russia, and the Pacific Isles; in England, Scotland, Wales, and throughout the entire length of this great confederacy; it professes already to number its proselytés by thousands, through the labors of their evangelists, who are continually swelling the ranks, and augmenting the resources of the great Zion in the West.

It was not long since suggested to me by an intelligent gentleman, that the rise of such an imposture as Mormonism, characterized by such an active propagandism, was proof of the weakness of the religious sentiment on the part of our people. Precisely the reverse of this appears the conclusion which should be reached. It is because the religious convictions of our people are so earnest, and the Christianity of our day is so aggressive, that it is burlesqued by such a religious fraud. A living writer in our own State, whose name is the synonyme of historic lore, has said: "There is no great working idea in history—no impulse which passes on through whole masses, like a heaving wave over the sea, that has not its own caricature and distorted reflection along with it." No religious movement, for example, was ever more earnest than the Reformation in the sixteenth century, and no movement was ever more marked by the grimaces of fanaticism, or travestied by the vagaries of enthusiasts. With this principle in view, it may not be risking much to say, that no age since that of the Apostles, could have given birth to such an imposture, marked by so much of missionary zeal, as the age which is most remarkable for the propagation of the Christian faith over the earth. Mormonism, in its propagandism, is truly an exponent of this age of Christian missions.

2. A second feature of the Mormon scheme, reflecting in a measure the age which gives it birth, is, *the refined communism lurking under its social structure, and the effort to build up its power by*

means of emigration. When the ambition of Mohammed enlarged from that of a reformer to the founder of an empire, he resorted to the only policy which, in those times, could avail him. The sword alone could open the path to glory and to power; and in all the empires of those rude and warlike ages, every stone was cemented with human blood. Mohammed, in becoming a military chieftain, simply yielded to the spirit of his countrymen; and Joseph Smith, equally unconscious of the controlling influence of public sentiment, unwittingly becomes the exponent of his age. Colonization takes now the place of conquest. The spirit of adventure, which once clad the knight errant in his steel armor, now pushes the emigrant forth to drive his plough through the broad acres of waste territory which every where on this continent invite his entrance. The tide of emigration continually pouring from the older settlements, soon peoples the wilderness, which begins to blossom under the husbandman. Thus, State after State is added to the Confederation, with a rapidity which attests the truth that empires are now built of colonies; the plough and the loom having supplanted the sword and the battle-axe. It has been already stated that the first development of the Mormon scheme contemplated the founding of a colony, embracing all the converts to the new faith. Joseph Smith did not, it is true, cast his eye beyond the borders of civilization; which is shown from the tenacity with which the sect clung to their early settlements in Missouri and Illinois. But in every location, the same social organization is preserved; and perhaps a more skillful and refined species of communism was never projected. The rock upon which socialism usually splits, is the entire denial of individual property. The destruction of this great principle of cohesion disintegrates society, and causes it speedily to fall apart. Joseph Smith has adroitly adjusted these opposite poles of individualism and communism, so that they reciprocally act. A tenth of all property, of time, of labor and of income, is paid into the general treasury, and is expended upon such works as the public interest may demand. Labor is a cardinal virtue of the system; and a drone is driven from the hive by the pressure of universal contempt. While a strict general supervision is exercised over the industry of all, room is granted to individual enterprise by the recognition of individual possessions. The most alluring rewards are held out to the proselytes, particularly to those of the old world. The offer of land fora sum that will cover the cost of surveying and recording, is a powerful inducement to the peasants of Europe; who are accustomed to look upon the owners of the soil as a superior class, into whose privileges they can scarcely hope to be admitted. This will serve to explain in part the success of Mormon missionaries in England and Wales; where the converts are reputed as being many thousands, waiting their opportunity to remove to the Canaan in the far west, which their fancy has painted. No part of this scheme displays greater practical wisdom than the formation of a colony in a country where land may be had for the settling; and the call made upon the laborers, colliers, mechanics, and factory slaves of over-crowded Europe to swarm to the new hive. It was no rude device too, while the temporal advantages are such as to attract adventurers in an age of emigration, to exact such a per centage as should maintain the community; as should bring the whole labor of all under a measure of control; and make each citizen a share-holder in the public wealth.

3. To a philosophic observer, probably the most striking feature of Mormonism, is, *the attempt to realize the conception of a Theo-democratic government.* It is a mistaken supposition that the ground-doctrine of every imposture is necessarily false; it is, on the contrary, oftentimes sublimely true. Indeed, it is this basis of truth which gives to imposture its formal character,—that specious appearance by which it is able to deceive. Fanaticism looks through a dense medium of prejudice and passion, and confounds the distorted image of truth with truth itself; and totally miscarries in the attempt to embody the speculative truth in a practical and tangible system. The fundamental postulate, for example, of the Fifth-Monarchy men in the 17th century, that God is the true Governor of nations, and the best administration is that which most perfectly conforms with the Divine will, is one of the most unquestionable and sublime truths ever enunciated. But no sooner did they attempt to apply this doctrine to actual life, and to realize the abstract idea in some concrete form, than the grossest fanaticism disclosed itself. The State must be entirely merged into the Church, the magistracy destroyed, the validity of human laws denied; and wholly mistaking the nature of spiritual liberty, they made it to consist in the possession of an inward spirit, wholly irresponsible to civil tribunals. The climax of fanaticism was reached, when they assumed to be the vicegerents of the Deity, and mistook their own lawless desires for "the inspiration of the Almighty."

The doctrine of a Theocracy is nothing new in the history of opinions. Indeed, the Mormons claim to stand in the same relations to God, as the Israelites under Moses. The civil jurisdiction is in the hands of church officers, from the inferior justice of the peace up to the governor.—The Justice is a bishop of a ward in a city, or of a precinct in the country; the Judges on the bench are constituted from the High-Priests, from the Seventies, or from the Apostolic college; and the highest functionary of the State is the President of the Church, who rules by virtue of his prophetic functions as the seer of the Lord. It is the revival of theocracy in our country which excites the wonder of the curious. And who can say, but it may be the reaction of mind against the avowed and boasted atheism of our own government? In the effort to put an eternal divorce between church and state, we seem to have fallen upon the other extreme. 'There is in our constitution a studied silence as to the providence and government of God. I do not mean to affirm that Joseph Smith ever reasoned upon this singular defect in our political constitution, and that he brought forward his theocratic doctrine in formal rebuke and opposition to it. There are currents and counter-currents in the opinions of men, the ebb and flow of which may be sufficiently apparent, while their reciprocal influence and inter-action may be wholly concealed. Without taking the shape of a logical statement, the religious sentiment may feel this want of recognition of the Supreme Ruler. If, at a future day, these theocratic pretensions of Mormonism should give trouble to our government, serious persons will scarcely be able to avoid the reflection that somewhat of rebuke, if not of retribution, is intended for practically ignoring the existence and control of Almighty God.

But the impress of the age is most visible in the union of democracy with theocracy; a combination scarcely conceivable, except by minds trained in the political schools of this country. It is very singular that governments the most absolute and despotic are often administered in the most democratic spirit. Strong affinities may exist between rulers and subjects, when the class of the former is continually recruited from the ranks of the latter. In the Mormon scheme, the complexity of its polity and the number of offices open many doors for the admission and elevation of ambitious men: and the absence of hereditary rule prevents that wide interval of rank and intercourse, which obtains in all countries where the government is not elective. The democratic spirit thus pervades a Hierarchy, which, in its essential constitution, is an unlimited despotism. lt is, however, an odd application of the democratic. principle, which could not have been dreamed of, except in this democratic age and country, that by the vote of his peers a man should be designated to the office of a seer; and thenceforward obeyed with absolute submission, as the oracle by which the decrees of Heaven are infallibly conveyed.

4. Mormonism has been already represented as a relapse into the old civilization of Asia, by the re-introduction of Polygamy, and the consequent depression of the softer sex. I should not omit to notice the bold effort *to invigorate that stiff, inert civilization, by infusing the spirit of modern progress.* Without wandering at will in the enticing field of comparison between ancient and modern civilization, the terms just employed express the distinguishing traits of the two. The former was stationary, the latter is progressive: the one stereotyped,

presenting at all times the same leaden aspect, dull, monotonous and stiff; the other, ever-changing, its elements in perpetual ferment, and marked by new developments as the result of the ceaseless struggle. In Mormonism, we discover at least three influences which made Asiatic civilization so inert and uniform. The first of these is the degradation of woman; for degraded she is, the moment she sinks from the side of man as his friend and equal, and takes the veil of seclusion in the harem of a master, the minister of his pleasures. Mormonism stamps the brand of social inferiority upon her, by merging her, even in the estimation of the Deity, in the person of her husband, and giving her no other consideration save (to use their own language) as she "raises up a holy seed to the Lord." Thus, by a single stroke of the pen, does Mormonism throw back half the race into a position from which it is impossible to ascend: and to retard the intellectual and moral advancement of those who are constituted by nature the educators of mankind, all history shows is but to lock the wheels of social progress.

The second influence at work in the Mormon scheme, repressing its civilization, is, the merging of the individual into the system; making him, as one quaintly expresses it, only a single spoke in a great wheel; of no individual value, save as he is a component part of a great whole.—I need not pause to show how clear a trait this is of ancient civilization,—the glory and the liberty of the State were the glory and liberty of the citizen: but he had no existence, even in his own thoughts, independent of the commonwealth. We have only now to examine the complex polity of the Mormon government, to see how the ties are multiplied, which bind together the units of society. We have only cursorily to read the history of the sect, to discover how the glory of the Latter-day Church is the attracting power holding each atom to its place in the great orb.

The third element of fixity in Mormon society, is its theocratic government. In all the past, wherever theocracy prevails, society is benumbed as by the electric touch of the torpedo. It necessarily draws the line of caste between the People and the Priests,—the subject and the ruler. It moulds all classes and ranks after the same artificial type; it represses all those counter-influences which ruffle the face of society, and prevent stagnation; and over-awes investigation necessary to progress, by parading always before the mind its own Heavenly sanctions. "A certain portion of truth," says Mr. Guizot on this point, "is doled out to each, but no one is permitted to help himself,—immobility is the character of its moral life; and to this condition are fallen most of the populations of Asia, in which theocratic government restrains the advance of man." In Mormonism, this influence is rendered more intense by its claim of progressive revelation. Not content with crowning itself with the awful majesty of a Divine origin, it asserts the high gift of perpetual intercourse with the Deity. With all the avenues of private judgement and personal discovery of truth thus effectually closed, the miserable victims of this pious fraud, "obedientia fracti animi et abjecti et arbitrio carentis suo," yield in passive submission to the assumptions of a crafty Priesthood, or to the stronger will of a single tyrant.

On the other hand, Mormonism has striven to engraft upon this stationary and inert civilization of antiquity the progress which so peculiarly distinguishes this age of discovery. The most liberal arrangements are made for education. Besides the primary schools under public control and inspection, the outline has already been drawn of a thorough University course. All branches of knowledge are to be taught; all living spoken languages are to be studied; the natural sciences are to be diligently prosecuted; practical astronomy, engineering, mechanics, the science of agriculture,—in short, all that can be learnt, whether for the purpose of ornament or use, are to be embraced in the extensive curriculum of study. A new feature of the system is the institution of a Parents' school for heads of families; so that at no point in life is education necessarily arrested. Even here, however, the fanaticism of the sect breaks forth. Scientific revelations from Heaven are to be enjoyed, no less than religious: and by this means, as complete a revolution is to be accomplished in the one kingdom as in the other. A new theory of astronomy has already been announced; and the Newtonian theories of gravitation, attraction and repulsion, are already said to be overthrown. In these efforts to suborn and corrupt science into a lying witness for their religion, we see a visible impress of the age upon the system. Here then is Mormonism under a double set of influences: the one setting it to spin and hum, like a boy's top, forever on the same spot; the other sending it forward upon a career of improvement to which there is no goal. Which shall finally be in the ascendant, their Prophet has not told us. Philosophers say that the harmony of the material universe is due to the antagonism of forces; and the adjustment being a product of Divine wisdom, may never be disturbed. But in a system which man has contrived, this harmony cannot always be preserved. Certainly there are warring elements in the Mormon imposture, which must produce a dreadful catastrophe, whenever the balance shall once be destroyed.

5. The last peculiarity in Mormonism which I shall now mention is its *transcendentalism*; though, to exhibit this trait fully, would require a minute analysis of its whole philosophy. As Smith never received a scholastic education, and never enjoyed leisure for general reading, this feature of his system would be utterly unaccountable, if it were not for the silent and insensible diffusion of knowledge and opinion. Those speculations, which can be originated only by minds of the highest order, percolate through others of far inferior grade; until at length the lowest stratum becomes saturated with opinions, the source and compass of which are but little known and appreciated. 'There are, in the Mormon belief, two self-existent principles: to one of which is assigned the name of intelligence; and to the other, the name of element, or matter. The origin of the universe is thus explained: in the far eternity, two elementary particles of matter consulted together and compared intelligences,—these called in a third atom, and united in one will, became the first power. From this intelligence, a God was begotten. This lays a foundation for one of the prime articles of their creed in regard to God, that he is not "a spirit without body, parts or passions;" but on the contrary, that he is material, having both body and parts. "It is impossible," says their chief theologian, Orson Pratt, "to show the least difference between the idea represented by nothing, and the idea represented by that which is unextended, indivisible, and without parts, having no relation to space or time." Having established this identity of definition,

he adds, "therefore an immaterial God is a deified Nothing, and all his worshippers are atheistical idolaters." He presents six definitions, in exposition of his idea of nothing: "Space is magnitude susceptible of division: a point is the negation of space, or the zero where it begins and ends. Duration is time susceptible of division,—an instant is the negative, or zero of duration. Matter is that which occupies space, between any two instants, is susceptible of division and of removal. Nothing is the negative of space, of duration and of matter, and is the zero of all existence." I give this as a specimen of the transcendental reasoning of this school. "In thus identifying the Deity," says the writer from whom these extracts are taken, "with nothing, an instant and a point, the Mormon has reached a conception of the most abstract being, and has made an affirmation of which an Euclid or a Hegel might be proud"—"of being in itself, which is the basis, the boundary, the origin, and the terminus of all; at once the zero of all existence, and the plenum,—and has reached the leading postulate of Hegel, that '*being and nothing is the same!*'" You will not, of course, call upon me to explain anything of all this: how, then, should it be transcendental? It is enough that I call upon you to observe how extremes meet: this untaught school of fanatics in the wilds and fastnesses of the Rocky mountains joining hands with the most unintelligible school of German meta-physicians.

But, if God be material, and was generated, there is no reason why he should not advance from lower to higher degrees of perfection. The hearer is perhaps prepared to learn next that God, the Father, like Christ, was once a man upon the earth,—that he died and rose again,—that he worked out his kingdom, and advanced so far in his faith, intelligence and power, as to become, in comparison with us, the Infinite. Further, if the Deity was generated, it does not shock us to learn that human souls were not made, but begotten; and that by the same obedience and faith, they too will advance to higher perfection, and at least possess the same dominion, property, power and glory, now enjoyed by the Deity, whose dominion will be proportionally increased: all which sounds very much like the development theory of a certain modern meta-physico-religious school, only a little run mad. Let us, however, go back for a moment to the seed of all these transcendental notions, the eternal existence of atoms which come together and compare intelligences; and we are thrown again upon the old whimsical theory that the earth is a great animal, endued with life;—only Mormonism goes beyond this in absurdity, and makes it capable of knowledge; and "the earth itself, even its minerals and metals, and all creation is alive."

The transcendental spirit of this strange system is also seen in their idea of faith, which they consider an attribute of God as well as of men. It is "the will, the principle of action, in all intelligent beings, exercised for acquiring glory and accomplishing holy works." In the Deity no less than in the creature, it is "the great governing principle, which has power, dominion and authority over all things."

'he next and last peculiar doctrine which I shall adduce, not only illustrates the transcendental tendencies of this superstition, but also the adroitness with which its founder addresses it to the strongest affections and holiest sentiments of the human heart. Starting with the postulate that things earthly are modelled after the pattern of things celestial, he connects closely the two worlds. As long as the probationary state shall continue on earth, there is a corresponding probation afforded to spirits in the other world. Upon this is founded their doctrine and practice of baptism for the dead. The living become proxies for the dead,—are baptized and fulfil all righteousness in their stead. 'These are hereby admitted to salvation, and are added to the house-hold of the surety at his resurrection, augmenting his train. Naturally, from this view of probation in the spirit-world, flows the doctrine of Metempsychosis, almost in the old Brahminical sense. As the souls begotten of God had originally the choice to remain as they were, or to take a material body, and ascend by obedience to greater glory and power; so, if they fail in the first probation, the soul takes a lower tabernacle, pays the forfeit for its offences, and retraces its steps to celestial glory. It is needless to show how this doctrine takes possession of the sympathies of the soul, at that moment when the rupture of earthly ties causes the heart to bleed, and the remembrance of the dead is a holy exercise of the soul.

I need not enlarge these remarks. Enough has been said to show that Mormonism, not content with the transcendentalisms of its own age, has adopted all the strange dreams of the mystics in past ages. We have the ancient Hindoo myth respecting God and the universe, almost literally re-produced; the gnostic theory of emanations is given us in the generation of human souls; the Pythagorean dogma of transmigration is presented almost without modification; while the sympathy of living and departed spirits, and the attendance of one upon the other, is but the wild notion which underlies the spirit-rappings of the present day. It is, in short, a strange composition of all the pantheism and mysticism in all periods of the world, with a strong tincture of the peculiar metaphysics of the age which gave it birth.

It would not be wholly uninteresting now to scrutinize he tortuous lines in the palm of this coarse imposture, and prognosticate its future. But, apart from the peril that attends all predictions, I am warned by the sands of the hour-glass not to enter upon any new line of thought. We cannot fail to glean, from the rapid survey which this lecture has taken, the elements of decay which must eventually work its overthrow. The liberal course of education which they are projecting cannot but open the eyes of the inquiring to the extravagance of their superstitions: and the effort to corrupt science, and to push their frauds into the kingdom of nature, must tumble the whole crazy enterprise to the ground. The weakening, too, of family ties, is in reality drawing away the very foundations and under-pinning of social order. History, when challenged, can give no other testimony in regard to polygamy than that it is a forcing-bed of vice. What institution could Satan himself devise, a surer nursery of crime, than a numerous house-hold, whose members are not held together by ties of natural affection, but rather estranged by the most fierce and consuming jealousies known to the human heart? 'Then consider the heterogeneous character of the population swarming to this great western hive, from the dark lanes, and crowded factories, and filthy collieries of the old world,—the sewerage and drainings of European population. For a time, an outward pressure will hold those elements in contact; but no sooner shall the difficulties be overcome which attend the subjugation of a new country, than the centrifugal force will be disclosed, and we shall see only the "disjecta membra" of this now rising empire. The consolidation of power in the hands of the Presidency and Priesthood, and the vast accumulation of wealth under their control, cannot but corrupt the government. The absence, too, of all constitutional checks to their power, and the fanatical pretensions to the Divine favour, will render the tyranny at last, only the more insolent and oppressive. It has only to become intolerable, and the day of revolution is at hand.

To these explosive elements within the system, add the immensely powerful influence of this great Republic, in assimilating all the parts, however extreme, over which it obtains control. In this most remarkable and auspicious power, lies the only hope of our government in its rapidly expanding jurisdiction. I have recently met with the statement, that the United States, with their territories and dependencies, cover ah area twice as large as that of the Roman empire, in its palmiest days, under Trajan and the Antonines: and it may assist us to apprehend the vastness of our territorial area, to know that now the United States own not less than one billion, three hundred and eighty-seven million, five hundred and thirty-four thousand acres of public land, to be thrown into market and in some way disposed of. The unwieldy bulk of the Roman empire was one of the many causes of its dissolution; but then Rome gained its empire by conquest, and held its distant possessions by the strong hand of military occupancy and rule. America, on the contrary, gains her empire by emigration and colonization.

New States form with a swelling population, and at once take on a republican government, assimilated to the great model which is before them, and very soon are incorporated into the same. The strength of this moral influence cannot be measured, as it moulds all the communities which organize over the entire continent. Mormonism will soon feel the pressure of this influence upon either side—as soon as States shall form upon the Pacific coast—and insensibly will she catch the spirit, and take the forms of truly republican institutions.

We cannot cast our gaze beyond the Rocky Mountains, and scrutinize the face of society collecting upon our extreme western coast, without a measure of anxiety for the unfolding future. Our country is certainly entering upon one of the grandest experiments it has ever been called to undertake, and is passing through the severest crisis it has ever been made to know. We cannot fail to observe the singular coincidence, that while a bold attempt is made by Anglo-Saxons themselves to reproduce the old civilization of Asia, and while a community has actually been founded upon that basis, a strong and copious tide of really Asiatic population has been pouring into our California territory. Take, as an estimate the fact that within three months of the past year seventeen thousand emigrants from China have sailed from three of her ports, most of whom are discharged upon our coast. What is to be the issue of this commingling of races on this continent? In the language of an American Senator on the floor of Congress, "the reunion of the two civilizations which, having parted on the plains of Asia four thousand years ago, and having travelled ever afterwards in opposite directions around the world, now meet again on the coasts and islands of the Pacific ocean." Will the issue be in accordance with the fond prediction of the same Senator, "the equalization of the condition of society, and the restoration of the unity of the human family?" Time alone can declare—but we cannot be insensible to the momentous crisis which is before us, nor be indifferent, as we see the elasticity of our government subjected to severer tests than its framers ever dreamed. If it shall succeed, by its immense moral power, in moulding and casting to its own shape and form that stubborn civilization of past centuries, which it now touches so closely, it will discover a life which the history of four thousand years denies of every other government—and republicanism will come forth, amidst the acclamations of the world, to receive the chaplet of triumph, which shall forever adorn her brow.

www.ingramcontent.com/pod-product-compliance
Lightning Source LLC
LaVergne TN
LVHW050947080826
845145LV00004B/1440
* 9 7 8 1 6 3 1 1 8 6 3 7 0 *